CARING FOR YOUR HAMSTER

How to care for your hamster and everything you need to know to keep them well

WRITTEN BY VETERINARY EXPERT

DR. GORDON ROBERTS BVSC MRCVS

Hello! My name is Gordon Roberts and I'm the author of this book. I hope you enjoy all of the specialist advice it contains. I'm a huge advocate of preventative care for animals, and I'd love to see more pet owners taking the time to research their pet's health care needs.

Being proactive and educating yourself about your pet's health now, rather than later on, could save you and your pet a lot of trouble in the long run.

If you'd like to read more of my professional pet care advice simply go to my website at http://drgordonroberts.com/freereportsdownload/.

As a thank you for purchasing this book, you'll find dozens of bonus pet care reports there to download and keep, absolutely free of charge!

Best wishes,
Gordon
Founder, Wellpets

Contents

~

Introduction

Chapter 1:
About the Hamster

Chapter 2:
Hamster breeds and varieties

Chapter 3:
Choosing a hamster

Chapter 4:
Preparing for your hamster

Chapter 5:
Your hamster's arrival

Chapter 6:
Taming and handling your new hamster

Chapter 7:
Your hamster's diet

Chapter 8:
Hamster health

Chapter 9:
Hamster FAQs

Introduction

~

Have you decided you want a hamster in your life? You're not alone. Around the world, millions of people are keeping these cute creatures as pets. Not only are they small and adorable, they're also great fun for children, and don't take up a lot of space in the home. This doesn't mean that they're low maintenance though; if you want to own one of these little pets, you're going to need to prepare yourself for the work that comes along with it. Cages need to be cleaned regularly, food and bedding need to be bought, and the hamster is going to need lots of TLC from you on a daily basis. Once you're ready to take on these responsibilities, this book will guide you through the journey of looking after your first hamster. Hold on tight – it's going to be a fun ride!

Chapter 1:
About the Hamster

The humble hamster may be small, but he is far from insignificant. In fact, hamsters belong to the second largest family of mammals in the world, the cricetidae family, which has over 600 species throughout Asia, North and South America, and Europe. The hamster's biological siblings include lemmings, voles, rats and mice. Here are some more things you should know about the hamster before you decide to keep one as a pet.

Hamsters in the wild

It's important to realise that the hamster has wild ancestors and was not always kept as a family pet. These days, hamsters are rare in the wild, but they do exist. Their natural habitat is the dry, arid landscape of the Middle East and Southwest Europe. Syrian hamsters are the most common hamster alive today, and they do come from Syria, where the land is mostly desert.

This is a harsh environment for a small creature to survive in; the days are very hot and the nights can be extremely cold. The ground is covered with rocks or sand dunes. Of course, not all hamsters originate from Syria; some varieties are from Mongolia, for example, and some are from Siberia. All varieties have one thing in common: they must withstand extreme temperatures, harsh landscapes and a scarcity of food. So, these little rodents need to be very resourceful.

Nocturnal creatures

To avoid the heat of the day, and to be less visible to predators, hamsters have evolved to be nocturnal. This means that they sleep during the day, avoiding the risk of getting scorched in the sun. Once the sun goes down and the temperature falls, hamsters wake up and leave their burrows to find food. They typically spend around six to seven hours out in the open, above ground.

Often they will roam vast distances in search of food and water, which is why you'll see pet hamsters running for hours on their exercise wheels as if their lives depended on it. In the wild, they simply must have the energy to run in order to survive. As you can tell, with all of these wild instincts still evident, the hamster is no ordinary pet. If you're going to own a hamster you need to respect its nocturnal sleep cycles, and its need for lots and lots of exercise.

Varied diets

Hamsters in the wild eat a huge variety of foods – they aren't picky! Some wild hamsters have been known to eat insects, frogs, lizards and other small creatures they can find. Pet hamsters like a rather more conventional diet which includes seeds, grains, nuts, corn, fruit and vegetables.

Pouches as pockets

One of the most clever adaptations we can see in the hamster is the presence of two pouches or cheeks on either side of the mouth. Can you guess what these are for? They act as pockets to store food in! As the hamster tends to roam long distances in the wild, it picks up food whenever it can and stores it in the pouches to bring back to its burrow and eat later. A wise move, considering how many predators there are in the open.

Pausing for a quick snack could prove fatal. Having its own food stash at home also comes in handy during the day time, when the hamster won't venture out into the heat of the day. The word "hamster" actually refers to this behaviour, and comes from the German word "hamstern" which means to hoard. Even in captivity, hamsters are excellent little hoarders and you'll usually find a hamster's nesting box full of old food when you go to clean out the bedding.

The first hamster pioneers

Whilst there are many different species of hamster, the very first species to be domesticated was the Syrian hamster, or the Golden hamster, as it is sometimes called. The Syrian hamster was discovered back in 1797 by a man called Alexander Russell. He wrote about these strange new rodents in a book called The Natural History of Aleppo. Decades later, the golden hamster got its official name from the curator of the London Zoological society, George Robert Waterhouse. But how did the hamster make it all the way from Aleppo in Syria to our homes in Europe and America?

Well, in 1930, a zoologist from Israel, Aharoni decided to lead an expedition to Syria with the aim of finding golden hamsters. A local by the name of Sheikh El-Beled helped him to dig up a wheat field and in that wheat field they managed to find a golden hamster with her 11 babies. They were nestled eight feet into the ground in their tiny burrow. Needless to say, the mother hamster was quite alarmed at being scooped up and put into a box with her young. If a mother hamster feels her young are in mortal danger, she will often kill them herself before predators get to them and sadly, that's what she did with one of her babies. Aharoni decided to raise the remaining 10 babies by hand. Six of these youngsters managed to escape during the time they were in captivity, leaving four behind for breeding.

These early hamsters were successfully bred and before long there were enough to send to various zoos and institutions around Europe and the UK, including London Zoo. By the mid-1930s they were so popular that people had started to keep them as pets. In 1971, more hamsters were discovered in Aleppo and were sent to American where they also eventually became family pets.

Sadly today the Golden hamster is a threatened species in the wild, though there are thought to be millions in captivity.

Chapter 2:
Hamster breeds and varieties

There are about 26 different species of hamster in the world today, each with their own unique characteristics. So, how do you go about choosing one as a pet? This chapter will explain the most popular hamster varieties and how they differ.

The Golden Hamster

Perhaps the most popular and the most well recognised of all the hamsters is the Golden hamster, or the Syrian hamster as he is sometimes called, after the country he originates from. These are the teddy bears of the hamster world, being slightly larger than a lot of other hamster breeds and therefore a bit more cuddly. In the wild they have a distinct golden colouring with grey and white areas. They really are beautiful! However, nowadays they can be found in a wide range of colours, from chocolate brown to grey, cinnamon and even tortoise shell. You'll also find long and wavy haired varieties which are much fluffier but also come with the added responsibility of grooming.

The Golden hamster differs from other hamster breeds because they are solitary creatures and don't like to live with other hamsters. If kept as a pair, they will usually fight. Females are larger and slightly more aggressive than males if challenged. The average Golden hamster measures between 5 and 7 inches long and lives for two to three years. They are slightly calmer than some of the smaller hamster breeds and because they're larger they are a little bit easier to handle.

Golden hamsters have special scent glands on their hips which they lick and moisten. They then mark out a trail with these glands by rubbing them on surfaces – a very good trick for a creature that roams long distances and can follow their own scent trails home again.

Fascinating fact: Many Golden hamsters are used in scientific research. For example, their nocturnal natures have made them popular subjects for studies in circadian rhythms, which track our natural behaviour in relation to certain times of the day. About 90% of hamsters used in scientific research are Golden hamsters, and the remaining 10% are other breeds.

Dwarf Campbell Russian Hamsters

These hamsters are very small compared to their Golden cousins. They grow to about 4 inches in length. They can also live in groups of the same breed and sex, provided the hamsters are all introduced to each other from a young age. On average, they can live for about two years in captivity.

These little guys are a bit more nervous than Goldens, and they will sometimes give a little nip if they feel threatened. You need to be very careful handling them; not only are they fragile, but their small size and speedy legs mean they can easily slip from your hands and run to the nearest hiding hole in the room. On the plus side, they are exceptionally cute!

This breed was named after W.C. Campbell, who collected the first hamster of this breed in Mongolia back in 1902. The breed is characterised by its dorsal stripe which runs the length of the back, and its grey colouring. In captivity, these hamsters can also be found in albino and sandy coloured varieties.

Like the Golden hamster, these hamsters are omnivores, xxwhich means that in the wild they will feed on both plants and insects. However, unlike the Golden, their numbers in the wild are plentiful and they are not endangered as a species. They can be found in parts of

China, Kazakhstan, Russia and Mongolia.

Campbell's Dwarf hamsters have their own special scent glands which are behind the ears. These glands are used to mark out their territories, and they also use urine and faeces to send messages to other hamsters in the area. They have evolved to withstand very cold temperatures by simply exercising a lot, which warms the body. Like the Golden hamster, they also have pouches which can be filled with food, right back to their shoulder blades.

One thing to be aware of is that Campbells are prone to diabetes, so you should always make sure that you get yours from a reputable, knowledgeable breeder and that there is no history of diabetes in your chosen hamster's bloodline.

Fascinating fact: It has been found that in the wild, there are significantly more female Dwarf Campbells than males. This is nature's way of ensuring the survival of the species, as the females can run faster than males and escape prey more easily.

Winter White Russian
(also known as Djungarian or Siberians)

These little hamsters are very closely related to the Dwarf Campbells, and the two are often confused with each other. However, one major difference in these hamsters is that their fur turns white in winter, which serves to camouflage them in the snow. They come in a few different colours including blue-black and blue-grey or sapphire.

Like their Campbell cousins, the White Russian can also live in groups of hamsters of the same sex, however, they can sometimes fight amongst themselves, so owners will need to monitor the groups carefully. Despite this, they are a little bit less nervous and nippy when it comes to being handled than their

Campbell counterparts. Although they are just as tiny and fragile, so the same level of care applies. For this reason, you will need to supervise children when they are handling them.

White Russians have a lifespan of about two years and measure about 3 to 4 inches in length. Their small size means that often people choose to keep them in tanks rather than wire cages, which can sometimes have too many gaps.

In the wild, these little creatures have a very pronounced moult and a change from their summer coats to their thicker white winter coats. However, hamsters kept in captivity tend to have less noticeable changes in fur thickness. You'll also notice that they have fur on their feet to protect them from the cold ground in their native habitats.

Fascinating fact: the White Russian hamster can be interbred with the Campbell's variety to produce a hybrid variety. Although this is quite a common practice amongst breeders, it isn't advisable because it can lead to congenital defects.

Roborovski

The Roborovski is even smaller than the other dwarf hamster breeds, and is also very active and a fast mover. They are very good at squeezing into the narrowest of spaces and holes, so be very careful if you live in an older house with lots of nooks and crannies. They need to be handled with care because of their tiny and speedy bodies, and as a result they might be more suitable for experienced hamster owners. Despite this, they don't tend to nip and can be tamed relatively easily.

This variety can also be kept in groups of the same breed and sex, and is quite sociable. The breed was first discovered by Lt. Roborovsky in 1894. They are native to Northern China, Mongolia, and Northern Russia. It's thought that the hamsters of this variety in the UK originate from a group of Roborovskis brought over from Holland in 1990.

These tiny hamsters measure just 2 inches long on average, though they have quite long legs in proportion to their bodies. They are the true dwarfs of the hamster world! They don't have the dorsal stripe of the other dwarf varieties mentioned here, but they do have very cute faces with white tummies and grey or brown fur on the rest of their bodies. Aside from this variety, there is also a Husky coloured

Roborovski which has a completely white face. This breed is extremely active and needs companions to run around and burrow with. Toys like tubes and tunnels are also a great idea. They love to burrow, so choose a material that's easy for them to dig into and a tank that is deep enough for them to make burrows down into.

Fascinating fact: Roborovskis have very efficient kidneys and their bodies are highly adapted to desert habitats. Their kidneys allow them to conserve lots of water and they produce very little urine.

Chinese

Whilst still technically a dwarf variety, the Chinese hamster is a little larger than his pint-sized cousins, to which he is only a distant relative. He is distinctly mouse-like, with the ability to cling to his owner's fingers when being handled, just like a dormouse would cling to a stalk of wheat. Adding to this effect is their longer more mouse-like tail and their slightly leaner build. In the wild, Chinese hamsters are brown with a black stripe running the length of their bodies. They have grey flecks and a white belly. In captivity the Chinese also comes in a white-spotted variety.

When they are young Chinese hamsters can be nervous, but once tamed they can usually be handled with ease and will be much calmer. Despite the cute exterior, Chinese varieties can be very territorial and as such, they are best kept individually rather than in groups or pairs. They are probably the least commonly kept pets of all the well-known hamster breeds. They grow to about 4 inches in size.

Fascinating fact: the Chinese hamster and other hamster breeds can catch colds from human handlers, so if you are ill you should avoid handling your little friend.

Chapter 3:
Choosing a hamster

Since you now know a little bit more about what types of hamsters are out there, you should have a fair idea of what kind of hamster you'd like. This chapter will help you make some other important decisions in the run up to bringing your hamster home, including where to get your hamster and what kind of housing you'll need.

Is a hamster right for you?

Before you go running off to the pet shop in search of your perfect hamster, you need to decide whether a hamster really is the pet for you. Hamsters are unique pets that need just as much care and attention as any other small animal. Here are some areas you might want to think about before you make your final decision.

Are my children old enough for a hamster?

Over the years, the hamster has slowly gained a reputation as a children's pet, and they are usually given as a first pet to kids who may be asking for something bigger and more costly such as a puppy. Whilst hamsters make fantastic first-time pets for children, you need to be aware that they are small, fragile and can easily go missing if they escape or are allowed to roam free.

Children should first be educated on how to handle a hamster and what is acceptable behaviour with these small creatures. For example, a child needs to be very calm when handling a hamster or they will get nipped, which may result in them dropping and possibly injuring the hamster. Once the hamster drops to the ground he will most certainly run for the nearest hiding place, and can then take hours to capture again. So, very young children are not suitable for hamsters. A child over eight or nine years old will be a better candidate, since they will have learned a little bit more about animals, and how to treat them.

Bear in mind also that these little creatures only live to two or three years old, so the child will need to be prepared for that sad inevitability. However, with that said, a hamster can be a great way to teach your children the responsibilities of feeding, cleaning and caring for an animal.

Do I have a suitable home for a hamster?

Firstly, the ideal home for a hamster is one where there are no cats or dogs. Hamsters frighten easily, and are also seen as prey by larger animals. Even if you think your cat or dog can be relied on to behave around a hamster, you should never put them in close contact with each other. It's not fair on the hamster and it could end in tears.

Secondly, your home needs to be one that is relatively quiet during the day, so that the hamster can sleep and live out his naturally nocturnal lifestyle. Children need to be educated about this too – it's not fair to disturb a sleeping hamster just because a child wants to play with him.

Lastly, if you're going to let your hamster out to exercise, you need to be extremely careful about where you do it. Hamsters are master Houdinis, and can fit into the smallest gaps and holes. They can chew on wires and have been known to gorge themselves on carpet corners, too.

They will also go to the toilet wherever they see fit, and empty their pouches of food if they feel they've found a good hiding place. So, if you're going to take the risk of letting your hamster run around, choose a room where there is no carpet, cables or small nooks and crannies to hide in.

The bathroom might be a good place to try. Really though, if your hamster has an exercise wheel in his cage then he shouldn't need to run free. Hamsters will run miles on their wheels each night when given the chance.

Can I commit to looking after a hamster?

Even if your kids lose interest in the hamster, you must be there to clean the cage and feed it. Hamsters aren't low maintenance – they need attention and care to make sure they live healthy, happy lives. Cages especially can start to smell if left for too long, and your hamster is sure to fall ill if he is left more than a week in a dirty cage. So, be prepared for these aspects of hamster care. You'll also need to invest in bedding, food, and veterinary treatment whenever it's needed.

Where to get your hamster

Now that you've thought through all of the above, it's safe to say that if you're still reading this, you are serious about getting a hamster. Congratulations! The fun is only just beginning. Here are some places you can usually get hamsters from:

Breeders

Before you run off to your local pet shop, do a little bit of research to see if there are any breeders in your area. Hamsters born and raised in family homes will usually be a lot calmer and tamer than hamsters who have been raised in the impersonal setting of a pet shop. The babies will have been handled from a young age, and should be friendlier and less nippy than those that have had no human contact before.

Make sure any breeder you consider can provide you with a reference from someone who has owned one of their hamsters. They should also be able to tell you all about your chosen hamster's breed and bloodline. If they can't tell you very much, they are probably an amateur breeder and you need to be especially vigilant in making sure their hamsters are healthy.

Ask to see the babies with the mother if possible, or if they have already been weaned, ask if you can see the mother anyway – just to check she is well looked after. In most cases, she will be but it pays to be sure. Since there is little profit to be gained from breeding hamsters, people usually do it for the love of the animals, so you won't find as many "bad" breeders as you will with, say, puppies for example.

Pet shops

Pet shops need to be approached with caution. You should pay a few visits to a pet shop over time to check on how the hamsters there are treated. For example, are they left out in draughty places? Are their cages cleaned regularly? Do any of them seem to be ill? Are they provided with enough space to move about in, and an exercise wheel? Do the staff know where the hamsters came from – were they bred in the pet shop or have they arrived from an outside breeder?

Bear in mind that a hamster from a pet shop may not always have had close contact with humans, so you may need to put in some extra work taming it once you get it home. Also, some of the more unscrupulous pet shops forget to wean their hamsters at the right time and as a result, you could end up taking home a female that has already fallen pregnant. Be sure to ask about all this before you make a purchase.

Pet shelters

If you're keen to re-home a hamster that's been abandoned or surrendered, then check your local pet shelter to see if they have hamsters. The advantage of these "pre-loved" hamsters is that they may already be tamed. You will also be doing a good deed by re-homing a hamster that really needs a loving family. Hamsters from pet shelters will have been checked over by a vet to make sure they are healthy enough to be re-homed, which is another advantage for you.

Choosing the right breed

In general, you should choose a Golden (or Syrian) hamster if you're looking for a single pet, that is going to be easy to handle. If you prefer to keep your hamster in a group and to watch them make their own fun in their cages, then one of the dwarf breeds mentioned in the last chapter may be more suitable.

How to choose the right hamster

Now comes the fun part: choosing the right hamster from a litter of pups. Here are some tips:

What to look for...
- A hamster with bright eyes
- A hamster that is active and agile
- A hamster with a healthy appetite
- A hamster that moves well, with no problems limping or moving in general
- Check that the hamster you have your eye on is fully weaned, meaning that they are old enough to eat solid food and be away from the mother

What to avoid...
- A hamster that is hunched up, which can be a sign of pain or illness
- A hamster that seems to be scratching a lot on one spot of skin
- A hamster with dull looking or sunken eyes
- Hamsters with runny faeces or faeces hanging from their fur
- Check the hamster has no signs of discharge coming from the nose, eyes or rear end, with no signs of sneezing, wheezing or coughing
- Check that the hamster, if old enough to reproduce, has not been living with hamsters of the opposite sex and is not pregnant as a result

Choosing a long haired hamster

Long haired hamsters have been purposely bred to have longer fur. The fur itself needs to be kept free from matts, and should ideally be groomed by you every few days. Long fur can be time consuming to look after, and it can also get caught in exercise wheels, or have faeces caught in it. So be aware of these aspects if you want to get one of these varieties. They look extremely cute, but they do require extra care and attention.

Should I choose a male or female hamster?

There are some conflicting opinions on which sex of hamster makes the ideal pet. Neither is the "better" one, but there are some subtle differences between them. For example, if you ever want to breed from your hamster you will want to get a female. If you want to avoid the risk of picking up a pregnant hamster from the pet shop, opt for a male.

Male Golden hamsters are slightly smaller than females, and some people report that they are more docile and easier to handle than females. Females hamsters go into heat every few days, which means their hormones fluctuate and they give off a slightly musky odour. This could be one reason why males are seen as calmer. Males tend to have slightly thicker fur, but they are also prone to fur loss as they age.

Should I get a baby hamster or an adult?
You can get either, but remember that if you get an older hamster you will not have as much time left with it, as hamsters only live for two to three years. Getting a young hamster of five to six weeks old or more might be a good idea, because younger hamsters are easier to

Chapter 4:
Preparing for your hamster

As the day of your hamster's arrival draws near, you'll need to make sure you're fully prepared to welcome him home. This chapter will go through some of the equipment you're going to need to keep your hamster happy, safe and healthy.

Choosing a cage for your hamster

There are lots of different hamster cages out there and each design has its own pros and cons. We'll go through the most common cage types below:

Wire cages

A wire hamster cage has thin metal bars and a plastic base. The bars make it easy for you to attach a water bottle or wheel, feed your hamster through the bars and also, your hamster will use the cage as his own climbing frame. Some hamsters are real dare-devils and like to scale the roofs of their cages too, so make sure there are different floors and levels so he doesn't fall from a height. These cages are very popular, especially for Golden hamsters, but you should be aware of the following:

- Some hamsters have been known to chew through the bottoms of plastic bases, so don't get a very cheap cage with thin plastic on the base. Try to get something good quality that will last.
- Hamsters will certainly chew on the metal bars of the cage, and eat any paint that covers the bars at the same time. It's not known whether this has any harmful effects.
- With metal cages, there is a risk that very small dwarf hamsters could squeeze through the gaps in the bars. They will also not get the opportunity to indulge in their love of burrowing, as these cages tend to have only shallow bases.
- Metal cages can let draughts in, so be sure that yours is placed somewhere warm, away from draughty doors or windows.
- Modern wire cages have several levels and little stairways between them, giving your hamster plenty of space to run and climb. Avoid the more old fashioned cages which are very small and only have one floor.

Cages with plastic tubes and tunnels

Nowadays you can buy space-age looking hamster cages which are made up of a series of tunnels, tubes and different compartments. Many of these cages allow you to buy add-ons so you can build them up over time. From a hamster's point of view, these are fantastic! They provide plenty of opportunities to run and climb through the network of tunnels, creating a similar habitat to the burrows they would use in the wild.

If you're going to get one of these ultra-modern enclosures, bear in mind the following:

- These cages have many different parts to them that you will need to assemble. There is always a risk with so many different attachments that one part will become loose and possibly fall off, leaving your hamster an opening to escape through. So, be sure that all the attachments fit properly and are strongly secured. Use duct tape if you're concerned.
- Because these cages have so many different attachments, they are a little bit more time consuming to clean. The best thing to do is soak everything in a bucket and then rinse each piece thoroughly before drying and putting it back together.
- You might find it a little bit more difficult to get hold of your hamster if he has so many tunnels and compartments to hide in, so be prepared for handling to take a little bit longer.
- These plastic compartments can get hot very quickly in the sun, and there is very little ventilation, so be sure your hamster's space age home is placed somewhere out of direct sunlight.

Tanks

A lot of people who are getting dwarf breeds of hamster choose a tank. This is because the smaller hamsters love to burrow. Glass tanks can be filled up with a deep layer of bedding so that the hamsters can make their own little tunnels and chambers. The glass in the tank allows you to see the tunnels and watch your little hamsters scamper through them.

Since many people get groups of dwarf hamsters and tend to watch them more than take them out for handling, this style of cage proves ideal. However, bear in mind the following:

- Hamsters need to run a good deal during their active hours, because they have so much energy to burn. The problem with tanks is that they are slightly less able to accommodate an exercise wheel which is one of the main ways hamsters exercise in captivity.

- However, if you get a larger tank and fewer hamsters, they should have more space to run.
- Tanks are probably a bit restrictive for Golden hamsters, which tend to be larger and need more exercise.
- You need to choose the material you're going to fill your tank with carefully. Some materials aren't suitable for hamsters. Sawdust, for example, might not be ideal for making tunnels in as it won't hold its shape.
- As with the plastic tunnel cages, tanks are usually not very well ventilated and this can lead to damp, warm environments where bacteria can spread. So, make sure the roof of your tank lets in some air, and be sure to clean out the tank regularly.

Buying the right bedding or substrate

Hamsters love nothing more than to curl up in a nest, and all the better if they can make a burrow leading to that nest. To create the ideal environment for your pet, you are going to have to choose your bedding or "substrate" (what you fill the cage with) carefully. It needs to be soft, comfortable, absorbent, and safe. Here are some choices to consider.

For the ground of your hamster's cage:

- Wood shavings: not the easiest for burrowing in, although they do absorb urine well.
- Saw dust: very absorbent, but probably a bit too fine and may get in your hamster's eyes and nostrils.
- Wood chips: be very careful with wood chips as they can splinter and harm your hamster. One safe type you could go for is Aspen shavings. Cedar and pine shavings should be avoided at all costs as they contain harmful chemicals that can make your hamster very ill.
- Wood and paper pellets: most pellets are safe to use, although they can make the cage very heavy.
- Soil and sand: Some people use a mixture of soil and sand, however, you need to make sure anything you put in the cage is completely free from bacteria, fungus and bugs. So opt for something

pre-packed that comes with these guarantees. There are many, many forums debating the pros and cons of soil bedding so have a look at those before making a decision.

For your hamster's nest:

- Shredded paper or tissue: as long as there is no ink on the paper, this is ideal and very safe for your hamster – it's also very easy to make at home. Newspaper should be avoided as the ink print is toxic to your pet.
- Hay: some people use hay, which is perfectly safe but you will need to make sure it doesn't come straight from the fields as fresh hay can contain mites and other insects. Straw is not safe as it is too sharp and can hurt your hamster's delicate eyes.
- Synthetic wool: Avoid this, and any other wool type bedding as it isn't safe for your hamster to ingest and can cause choking.

Important tips for substrates and bedding:

- Make sure you choose bedding and substrates that are free from chemicals, dyes and artificial odours – all bedding must be as natural as possible
- Make sure any nest bedding is safe for your hamster to ingest – often hamsters will stuff bedding into their pouches to make nests with.
- Wherever possible, choose bedding materials that have been made specifically for hamsters, rather than any other pets. Hamsters have their own set of needs.

Equipment for your hamster's cage

Now that you have your cage and bedding sorted out, it's time to fill your hamster's cage with the accessories he needs. Here are some you should buy:

- Food bowl: Get a good ceramic food bowl that your hamster can't tip over or chew to pieces. Ceramic is very hygienic and will last a long time too.

- Water bottle or water bowl: Water bowls tend to get dirty or get tipped over easily, so they should really only be used if your hamster refuses to use a water bottle. You could start off with both a bowl and a bottle to see which one your hamster prefers.
- Something to gnaw on: Hamsters have teeth that grow continuously, and they need to file them down by chewing and gnawing on something hard. There are a few types of hamster chews ranging from wooden to stone – it's best to get something from the pet shop that's designed specifically for hamsters. Many people want to get a tree branch from their gardens, but there are no guarantees that a tree is free from bacteria and insects, so stick with the pet shop where possible.
- A nesting box: Hamsters love to curl up in nests where they feel safe and cosy. Choose an enclosed nesting box for your hamster with plenty of room for him to turn around and store food in. Fill it with shredded tissue paper and he will soon make it his own.
- A hamster wheel: If your cage doesn't come with a hamster wheel, buy one separately. Hamsters do a lot of running in the wild and are still only relatively new to being kept as pets. They need to run for a few hours every night. Make sure the wheel you choose is good quality and won't squeak or rattle in the middle of the night.
- An exercise ball: One great invention for those who don't want their hamsters running free throughout the house is an exercise ball, where your hamster is actually inside. Your hamster can still have that feeling of running large distances like on his wheel, but he'll also be able to see where he is going and move about your living room floor from the safety of this transparent ball.
- A carry case: For trips to the vet, you may want to invest in a small carry case or box. Cardboard shoe boxes can be used, but hamsters will chew through the cardboard.

Chapter 5:
Your hamster's arrival

Now that you have all the hamster equipment you need, you can bring home your new hamster. This section will give you some tips for the first few days of owning a hamster.

Transporting your hamster

Your little hamster is probably going to be stressed when making the journey from where he was raised to your home. To make things easier, you need to transport him in a safe, comfortable container. It should have:

- Air holes for breathing

- A durable material, preferably not cardboard which can easily get soiled or chewed during the journey
- Some soft, cosy bedding to make the journey comfortable
- Ideally, some bedding that was originally in your hamster's old enclosure, so that he has something that smells familiar around him for the first couple of days (you can take this and put it in his new nesting box later on).

Arriving home

It might be easier and kinder to pick up your new hamster in the late afternoon or early evening, so that you don't disturb his usual sleeping hours and routine.

Ask your pet shop or breeder to provide you with some of the same food your hamster has been eating all along, so that you don't have to abruptly switch his diet to something new on top of all the other new changes in his environment.

Once you get home, place the container at the entrance to the cage and get your hamster to walk into the cage by himself, if you can. This will minimise an already stressful situation by not forcing him to be handled just yet.

Make sure your hamster's cage is in a suitable area of the house. That means somewhere that:
- Is away from draughts and direct sunlight
- Is inaccessible to other pets
- Is peaceful during the day time when hamsters sleep
- Won't wake anyone up at night, when the hamster will be running on its wheel

The first three days

Most experts advise waiting a full three days before you try to handle your new hamster. This gives him time to get used to his new cage and to all the smells and sensations of your home without the stress of also being handled by someone new.

Remember, if you're switching your hamster from his old diet to the food you're planning to feed long term, you need to do it gradually to avoid upsetting his stomach and stressing him out. Mix the new food in a little more each day, and after about a week he should be eating only the new diet.

Chapter 6:
Taming and handling your new hamster

Once your little friend has settled into his new home environment, you can start the process of getting him used to being handled. Some people may be lucky enough to get a hamster that has already been tamed. If this is the case, you'll just need to get your hamster used to your smell. Usually though, a new hamster will need at least a little bit of careful taming before he gets really used to being handled. This section will help you to do that.

Choose the right time

It's unfair to your hamster to handle him when he's asleep. Instead, you should wait for him to wake up in the evening and have a go at handling him then. He will feel much more comfortable once he's fully awake and alert.

Being persistent

Before you begin trying to handle a new hamster, make sure your expectations are realistic. Not every hamster is going to enjoy being handled, but they will grow to tolerate it and pretty soon, they won't bat an eyelid.

Some hamsters take longer to become tame than others. Dwarf hamsters in particular are a little bit nervous and can nip. Don't let that put you off. Too many frustrated hamster owners simply give up and simply leave their hamsters in the cage to live out a wild existence.

This is a really bad idea, as it makes it really stressful for your hamster whenever he has to be handled – for example, if you bring him to the vet, or even if you need to move him to a container while you clean his cage. These situations are going to be tricky if your hamster isn't tame. It is very sad to see a hamster that never gets handled. So, make sure you keep going with the handling until your hamster is calm enough to climb onto your hands voluntarily. It will be worth it.

Staying calm

Above all, you need to stay calm when handling your hamster for the first time. One thing you could do if you're nervous is have a friend that has already tamed a hamster to visit, and help with the process.

Your hamster needs to have positive experiences of being handled from the very start, or he will grow to associate your hands with a bad situation. So, make sure you're in a calm, positive frame of mind before you begin. Having a "can do" attitude is important.

How to handle nipping

If you have a particularly nippy little hamster, you could wear gloves at the beginning if it makes you feel calmer. Once the hamster gets used to the idea of being held and walking on your hands, you can phase out the gloves.

Try some treats

If you want your hamster to feel distracted and maybe to associate handling with something rewarding, you can use treats at the very beginning. Some particularly tempting fruit or vegetables cut into tiny pieces should do the trick. At first your hamster might simply pile them all into his cheek pouches for later, but over time he will feel comfortable enough to stop and eat the morsels of food you give him. That's when you know you're making progress.

Choose somewhere with a soft landing

Before you take your hamster out and handle him, you need to choose somewhere safe to do so. That means somewhere with a very soft landing, like the couch. If you stand up when handling your hamster for the first time you are probably going to find he jumps out of your hands, or you get nipped and you drop him. You don't want him to have a huge fall when this happens. So, either sit on the carpet with your hamster's cage just in front of you or choose a large couch to put the cage on and sit beside it. It's also a good idea to choose a room that is secure, with all windows and doors closed and no nooks and crannies for an escaped hamster to hide away in. Make sure no one is going to walk into the room and interrupt you either – that could give you or your hamster a fright, or if your hamster is on the loose it could lead to him getting out of the room.

Step by step guide to handing

Here is a step-by-step guide to the very first time you try to handle your hamster. Good luck!

1. Begin by getting your hamster used to your smell. If you can put your hand inside the cage slowly without him flinching or hiding away, you are making progress. So, try to get to that stage before anything else. He should grow used to the idea that those giant hands of yours are nothing to be feared, and that they often bring gifts in the shape of delicious treats. Try spending an evening near the cage, putting your hand in at hourly intervals.

2. Get your hamster to the stage where he is brave enough to approach your hands. This might take you a couple of hours, or it might take a day or two. It depends on the hamster. Usually the best way to do this is to hold a small treat in the palm of your hand (inside the cage) and wait for curiosity to get the better of him. He will soon be at the stage where he crawls onto the palm of your hand to get the treat. Stay calm and still when he does. Repeat this several times over a few hours so he gets the idea.

3. Once you're sure your hamster is comfortable venturing onto your hand, you can progress to slowly moving the hand out of the cage when he is on it. This is much less stressful for him than being grabbed out of the blue. When you make a grab for a hamster it seems like an attack from a predator, so try to avoid this practice wherever possible. Instead, you should let your hamster make his way onto your hand in his own time, at least until he is properly tamed. Remember that we are trying to create only positive, rewarding experiences for your hamster so that he gets more and more comfortable with being handled. Your hamster might panic at this stage and jump off your hand back into the cage. If he does, don't worry. Just try again later.

4. When you can successfully move your hand (or hands) out of the cage with your hamster on them, you can then start to properly handle him. If both parties are calm, this should go well. Hamsters like to be constantly on the move, so don't expect yours to sit perfectly still on your hand. Instead, give him the chance to walk from one hand to the other and keep rotating your hands like a treadmill, putting one hand in front of the other and so forth. Don't give your hamster the chance to leap off – these are daring creatures and they will quite happily make the jump if they feel like it. Instead, always make sure your other hand is there in front of him so he can take his next steps. You will soon see him getting more and more active and faster on his legs. Hamsters tend to get more and more active the longer they exercise, so at the start of the handling session he will probably be slow and hesitant, but pretty soon he'll be racing along your hands.

5. Now it's time to get your hamster used to being picked up, rather than simply using your hands as an elevator every time. To do this, put him in an enclosure with an open top but that he can't climb out of, like the bath or a box with very high sides. That way, you'll be able to practice picking him up rather than having to tempt him out of the awkwardly shaped cage every time. Put a few distractions in the enclosure, like food and bedding, so he doesn't feel distressed. Then, simply use your two hands and cup them together. You are now going to scoop up your hamster with your two hands, gently – not too quickly, or he will get a fright, but not so slowly that he has the chance to climb out of your hands before you've moved them off the ground.

Why use the scooping method? It is probably the most gentle and least invasive way to pick up a hamster. Some people use more severe methods like pinching the scruff of the neck, or grabbing under the belly – these aren't necessary, and they aren't very nice for a fragile little hamster to experience.

Hamsters aren't toys and they shouldn't be handled roughly or carelessly – they are fragile creatures that need respect from their owners. Once you've spent thirty minutes to an hour practising this scooping method, your hamster should be at ease with it. There should never be any need to use a different method, unless your hamster is having his teeth clipped or being examined by a vet.

A word about children and hamsters

If you have young children, please don't give them the responsibility of taming their own hamster, especially if they haven't had a pet before. Children can be rough, and often get over-excited, forgetting that they are playing with a very real living thing that has delicate internal organs and can get frightened easily.

Please tame the hamster yourself before teaching your children how to handle it properly, and even then, please supervise your child until they are old enough to be trusted.

How to capture an escaped hamster

It is an inevitable fact that some day, somehow, your hamster is going to escape its cage or escape your grasp and run free somewhere in your house. When that happens, there are a few important things to do.

1. Alert everyone in the house that there is a hamster on the loose. Hamsters are so tiny that people need to watch where they are stepping.
2. Close all the windows and all the doors in the house. Each room should be sealed off to contain the hamster, even if you're not sure which room he is in.
3. Lock away any other pets immediately.
4. Now go to the room where you suspect your hamster is (if you don't know, simply follow these steps for each room one by one).
5. Spend a few minutes in the room sitting absolutely still and listening very carefully. When a hamster is on the loose you can usually hear it – eating carpet is a favourite activity, climbing curtains and even just running on the floorboards with its little feet can be heard. You might be lucky enough to catch a glimpse of him if you are vigilant enough.
6. Leave a particularly pungent smelling treat out in the centre of the room and sit nearby. Hamsters have an excellent sense of smell and it shouldn't be too long before yours comes running to see what tasty treat is there.
7. Once he's out in the open, you can drop a tea towel over him, a bucket or even a box. Then you can reach under it and pick him up. You can also try a long tube if you have one – hamsters love dark little hiding holes. Simply wait till he's entered the tube and then block the ends. If those methods fail, the National Hamster Council recommends setting up a humane trap and checking the trap first thing in the morning. Some escapees can take days or even weeks to be coaxed back into captivity, so don't give up!

Chapter 7:
Your hamster's diet

Congratulations! You have come this far and you're now ready to start a daily care routine for your new little friend. This chapter will go through the kind of diet your hamster needs in order to keep him happy and healthy.

Feeding your hamster

Once a day your little pet needs to be fed with fresh hamster muesli, which you can buy from the pet shop. Make sure the muesli you buy is good quality, with plenty of different nuts, seeds and grains included. You will soon see that your hamster has his favourite parts of the cereal, because the bits he doesn't like will be left behind! The best time to feed him is in the early evening, just before he wakes up. This will ensure that he doesn't wake up to old food, and that there is always something tasty waiting for him for breakfast.

Note: you should never feed your hamster cereal or muesli that has been made for human consumption; this will be far too sugary and filled with ingredients your hamster does not need. Stick to foods that have been produced specifically for hamsters.

Giving treats

In addition to his normal cereal, you can also add some treats to your hamster's menu. It's very easy to find things in your fridge that a hamster will eat (fruits, nuts and vegetables are always good ideas) so there should be no need to buy any of the processed, packaged hamster treats you'll see in pet shops.

Treats should be given only every few days; you don't want to upset your hamster's tummy by giving him too much fruit and veg in one go. Don't pile up the food bowl with treats, just give a few small pieces. Also bear in mind that some treats are going to be stored in your hamster's pouches and hoarded away in his nest box for later. You don't want this hoard of treats to build up and go stale. The RSPCA recommends scattering treats around your hamster's cage (avoiding the corners he uses as toilet areas) in order to mimic the foraging he would naturally do in the wild.

Here are some treats your hamster will probably love:

- Cucumber
- Carrot
- Apple
- Broccoli
- Pear
- Celery
- Blackberries
- Blueberries

- Banana
- Chicory
- Alfalfa
- Courgette
- Mange tout
- Green beans
- Cress
- Sweetcorn
- Sweet potato
- Turnip

Make sure all of the above treats are cut into tiny pieces that will be easy for your hamster to put in his cheek pouches. Also, wash everything thoroughly before giving to your hamster. Today's fruit and veg is treated with a lot of chemicals which could harm a tiny hamster.

Protein for hamsters

Hamsters are omnivores and in the wild they will eat insects. Whilst we don't suggest you do that, you can give your hamster a little bit of protein about once a week in the form of low fat cottage cheese or cooked pieces of egg. Nuts are also a great source of protein, but dwarf hamsters can get ill if they are given too many fatty foods, so always feed these treats in moderation.

Foods that hamsters can't eat

Make sure everyone in your family knows that they can't feed your hamster the following foods, as they are likely to make him very sick:

- Lettuce which can cause liver problems
- Onion
- Raw kidney beans
- Raw potato and raw potato tops
- Tomato leaves
- Rhubarb and rhubarb leaves
- Human foods like chocolate

Food safety

Don't guess what your hamster might be able to eat. Always check with your vet if you aren't sure. Here are some things to avoid:

- Food that is very sticky and can get stuck in cheek pouches, like peanut butter
- Overly sweet food, which can make hamsters diabetic (especially dwarf hamsters)
- Very fatty foods like full fat cheese can make your hamster ill

Old food

Every day, you should do a quick scan of your hamster's cage and nesting box and remove any food that is stale or has been there for too long. This will make sure your hamster doesn't eat anything that makes him ill, and it will also make his home a more hygienic place to live.

Water

Hamsters can go long periods without water, as they evolved as creatures that lived in harsh desert conditions. However, a hamster in captivity needs access to fresh water at all times. You should change the water in your hamster's bottle or bowl every day, even if you think it looks clean. Water that is left stagnant can go stale, and might also be a breeding ground for algae which is a green slimey substance that may harm your pet.

Supplements

There should be no need to give your hamster vitamin supplements as long as you are feeding him a balanced, varied diet of muesli and fresh foods. The only time you might need to give extra vitamin and mineral supplements is if your hamster is ill and your vet has advised you to. Giving large amounts of supplements can throw your hamster's system out of balance and may even make him feel worse. So, only give these under the direction of your vet.

Chapter 8:
Hamster health

Now that you're a fully-fledged hamster owner, it's time to familiarise yourself with hamster health in general. It's important to know the signs of illness in hamsters and also to know what is and isn't healthy – it could save you a trip to the vet some day. This chapter will give you the facts you need to know.

Healthy hamster checklist

Every time you handle your hamster, do a quick health check to make sure he is well and thriving. Here is a check list to go through:

- Eyes are bright, clear and alert
- Coat is healthy, glossy with no bald patches
- Skin has no sores, scaly patches or inflammation
- Body has no unusual lumps or bumps
- Hamster has not lost weight (bones will be easier to feel if so)
- Breathing is easy, with no wheezes or sneezes
- No discharge coming from the rear end, nose or eyes
- Ears are clean and clear of debris
- Movement is fluid with no limping or signs of pain
- Behaviour is normal, with no odd changes

Knowing the signs of illness

A good hamster owner knows the classic signs of illness, and is always vigilant for any of the following signs that something is wrong:
-
- Loss of appetite – food is left unfinished or untouched
- Excessive drinking from the water bottle (hamsters don't usually drink too much)
- Lethargy and listlessness when the hamster is normally active and

alert
- Hamster stays in the nesting box at times when it would usually be out and about
- Dull or sunken eyes
- Sitting in a hunched position rather than relaxed posture, which is a sign of pain
- Diarrhoea, or sticky, wet faeces which sometimes get matted in the fur
- Discharge coming from the nose, eyes or rear end
- Sneezing, coughing or wheezing
- A hard, swollen tummy
- Signs of injury, such as trailing a limb or limping
- Difficulty walking or seeming off-balance
- Scratching a lot on the same area of skin
- Abnormal bumps or lumps on the body
- Behavioural changes, such as suddenly not wanting to be handled, being unusually aggressive, or simply sleeping around the clock instead of waking up to exercise

Knowing when to visit the vet

The lists above should be very helpful in knowing whether to take your hamster to the vet. If you spot any of the above symptoms, you should book a vet's appointment as soon as you can.

Hamsters are so small and they don't make any noise, so hamster owners need to be very observant for signs of ill health that could easily go unnoticed. In particular, if you have children who normally handle your hamster, you should teach them about the signs above and what to look for.

Once a week, you should ask to look over the hamster yourself just to make sure he is healthy.

Common hamster diseases

In addition to knowing the signs of ill-health, you may want to be aware of the following common hamster illnesses:

Wet Tail

Every experienced hamster owner knows that wet tail can be very contagious. As the name suggests, this infection can cause watery faeces which cause the fur around the tail and bottom to feel wet. If you notice this in your hamster you should immediately separate him from any other hamsters in the group, and take him to the vet.

To be safe, if you keep a group of hamsters then they should all be seen by the vet to be sure. Normally though, wet tail affects the Golden or Syrian hamster more, and these hamsters aren't kept in groups. Vets usually treat this condition with antibiotics and fluids (your hamster may become easily dehydrated with diarrhoea). If caught early the condition can be treated and cured, but in more severe cases it can be fatal.

Bald patches and fur loss

If your hamster suddenly seems to have patches of fur missing, there could be a problem. Firstly, it could be that your hamster has mites, which are a tiny parasite that causes itching and a lot of stress. Your hamster will rub his body against the sides of the cage and will be persistently scratching and biting at the affected areas, causing the fur to fall out. Mites need to be treated by a vet as they cause your hamster a lot of discomfort and are also contagious between pets. So, the bedding and cage of a hamster with mites will need to be cleaned and disinfected thoroughly to kill all the mites.

You will need to do this very regularly whilst your hamster is being treated. Topical sprays are normally used, and if you have a group of hamsters the whole colony will need to be treated. Mange is another condition caused by mites, usually in the hamster's ears. They can cause an allergic reaction in your hamster leading to scabs and sores on the fur – a very sore and uncomfortable condition for your little pet. Creams, oral medications and injections can be used to kill off the mange, and any sores can be soothed with topical treatments.

Other causes of fur loss can be malnutrition, stress or fighting between hamsters that live in groups. Your vet should be able to make a proper diagnosis on examining your hamster.

Colds

Hamsters can catch colds from time to time, especially if they live in a cage that is kept somewhere damp or draughty. They can also catch colds from humans, so if you are ill, please don't handle your hamster until you are better! Avoid giving your hamster baths as this, too, can cause him to catch cold. Wheezing, sneezing and wet noses are all signs of a cold.

Keep your hamster somewhere warm and cosy and feed him some soft, vitamin C rich foods. If your hamster's cold seems severe you should take him to the vet as a cold can quickly develop into pneumonia in small creatures.

Red urine

Reddish coloured urine isn't always a sign of illness. Sometimes, it's caused by artificial dyes in your hamster's food. To be sure, you should change your hamster's diet and if the red urine doesn't go away, you will need to take him to the vet. Other causes of reddish urine include bladder stones, or an infection in the uterus called pyometra.

Pyometra

This infection of the uterus can be life threatening. It starts with bloody discharge and progresses over time until the hamster's uterus or abdomen swells to an abnormal size. Vet treatment should be sought as soon as possible.

Overgrown teeth

A very common problem that happens to hamsters is that their teeth grow so long that they can no longer eat. Often these hamsters haven't been given anything to chew on (such as a piece of wood or a mineral stone) that will file down the teeth. You might not notice anything is wrong until your hamster begins to lose weight and ignore much of the food in its bowl. This is because the teeth have made it too difficult to eat. A quick trip to the vet will confirm this, and your vet will clip your hamster's teeth back so that he can eat again. He may show you how to clip the teeth yourself at home, if you are confident enough.

Impacted pouches

Sometimes your hamster gets carried away and will try to store something in his pouches that really isn't suitable. Bedding is one common culprit. The result is that the item gets lodged in the pouch and the pouch becomes impacted. If you've noticed a familiar bulge in one of your hamster's pouches that stays there for more than a couple of days, there may be something stuck in the pouch that needs to be removed by the vet.

Conjunctivitis

If your hamster develops an allergy to his bedding, or if a tiny piece of debris gets in his eyes, he may show signs of conjunctivitis where the eye is red, inflamed and irritated. There may be discharge, and the hamster will rub at its eyes due to the irritation. Drops are available to treat these issues, and you should also look at changing your hamster's bedding if you think it might be causing an allergy. Sawdust is a common issue as the tiny particles of dust can easily get into the eyes.

Poisoning

If your hamster has come into contact with anything toxic, or he has accidentally eaten something harmful, he needs to go to the vet. Some substances which are toxic to hamsters include:

- Mouse or rodent poison
- Foxglove plants
- Chocolate
- Ivy

- Rhubarb and rhubarb leaves
- Oleander

Hibernation

In the wild, some hamsters will hibernate to get them through the harsh winters. Hibernation is when the animal goes into a very deep sleep and many of the usual bodily functions are put on hold, for example they will only wake up very occasionally to feed. Hamsters in captivity don't need to hibernate and usually they will not.

However, if they are particularly sensitive to the cold or are accidentally kept somewhere with no heating (not advisable under any circumstances!) they may go into hibernation as a natural reaction. If you believe your hamster is in hibernation, there is no need to disturb it (this might cause unnecessary stress). Simply make sure the room is nice and warm and there is plenty of fresh food and water left out for when he wakes. If the room gets warmer, he will wake up naturally in his own time.

Using the checklist

This list of hamster health issues isn't exhaustive, so don't rely on evidence mentioned here as a sign that you should visit the vet. In reality, anything odd or unusual (for example those symptoms listed in the checklist at the beginning of this chapter) should be cause for concern.

The good thing is hamster health care is usually not too expensive – these little animals are a lot cheaper to care for than dogs and cats. So you shouldn't feel worried about visiting the vet, even if it is for something minor. The chances are, your vet will be glad to see someone who takes such a keen, proactive interest in their pet's health.

Chapter 9:
Hamster FAQs

The last section will deal with some of the most commonly asked questions on keeping hamsters. Keep this book and refer back to this section whenever you need it.

How often should I clean out my hamster's cage? And how should I do it?

You should do a full clean of your hamster's cage at least once a week. Never leave it to the stage where it gets smelly, or where there are faeces everywhere. Your little hamster relies on you to keep his home clean and he will be very unhappy and unhealthy if left somewhere dirty. Some tips for cleaning out your hamster's cage include:

- Find somewhere safe to put your hamster while you're cleaning the cage. Bathtubs are often a good idea because your hamster can't climb out of them. Or, you could put him in his exercise ball if he is up and about.
- Start by emptying all of the sawdust out of the base of the cage. Then, empty out all of the bedding and old food from the nesting box.
- Disinfect everything from the cage base to the bars, the wheel and the food bowl, as well as the nesting box. Some cleaning solution in a bucket of hot water and a few wet cloths should do the trick. Clean the base until no trace of dirt or debris remains.
- Rinse everything you have just washed in fresh water, so that there is no trace of disinfectant left behind (it contains harmful chemicals which could affect your hamster).
- Dry everything thoroughly. Then, put down a fresh layer of paper in the bottom of the cage, and cover it with a couple of inches of sawdust (or whichever substrate you use). Tanks can be filled with a much deeper layer for burrowing. Put new bedding into the clean, dry nesting box and replace the clean food bowl with fresh food. Once the cage is back together, your hamster can be put back into his lovely clean new home.

Can I toilet train my hamster?

Believe it or not, some owners manage to successfully train their hamsters to pee in a particular spot in their cages. A little bowl filled with chinchilla sand is a good thing to try, or even just a shallow little box in the corner of the cage, so that the rest of the cage stays clean and dry.

Some dwarf hamsters can use a small jam jar on its side. Fill the toilet tray with some sawdust that has already been peed on and a couple of faeces. With a bit of luck, your hamster will soon get the idea that this is where the toilet is. Hamsters are very clean animals and usually go to the toilet in one corner of the cage anyway. This way, you can actually remove the soiled tray and replace it throughout the week, so that there is no smell in the cage between the weekly clean out.

Can I give my hamster a bath? How else can I keep him clean?

No, you should never give your hamster a bath. This would be too stressful for your hamster and he might catch a cold from it, which could be life threatening. If your hamster has something dirty matted in his fur, you can use a toothbrush to get it out, or you can simply clip away the soiled fur. Hamsters with long fur should be given a light grooming session with a little brush a few times a week.

My hamster has just had babies! What should I do?

It's not uncommon to get your hamster home from the pet shop only to find it has given birth a few days later. To prevent this, make sure you get your hamster from a place where they are separated into male and female groups from a young age.

Hamsters have a very short pregnancy of just 16-21 days. Before giving birth, your hamster will start to make a suitable nest for her babies and her belly will swell a few days before the pups are born.

Once she gives birth, you need to follow these guidelines:

- Don't touch the babies at all, until their eyes are opened and they are big enough to eat solid food (at least two weeks after they are born). If you touch the babies when they are young the mother may feel they are threatened and sometimes she will react by killing her own babies.
- Don't disturb the mother hamster. Make sure her cage is somewhere very peaceful and quiet, away from loud noises, other family members and pets. Resist the urge to peek inside the nesting box.
- Quietly and gently change the mother's food and water every day, but don't go near the cage otherwise. Don't try to handle her – she will not want to leave her pups and may become aggressive.
- If the babies stray from the nest, there is no need to move them –

the mother will usually do that when she finds them.
- If for any reason you absolutely must move the babies, use a barrier between your hands and the pup, so that the pup doesn't get your scent – otherwise, the mum might attack or reject the pup. Wrapping your hands in tissue paper is one thing you could try, or using a spoon rubbed in sawdust.
- Once the babies are three weeks old you can separate the male pups from the female pups in separate cages to prevent them from fighting or mating.

My hamster gnaws at the bars of his cage for hours

Hamsters that do this are usually bored, frustrated, or looking for something to chew on to file down their teeth. Here are some things to try:

- Get your hamster some toys to play with instead
- Make sure there is something such as a piece of wood for your hamster to chew on
- Get a bigger, more exciting cage for your hamster
- Try a tank-style hamster cage instead, where your hamster can burrow if he is bored
- Make sure your hamster has enough exercise which will keep him calm and happy – why not try a hamster ball in the evenings to tire him out?

You should never try to coat the bars of the cage with any deterrent, as this will just harm your hamster and it won't get to the root of the problem.

Can I add a new hamster to my group of dwarf hamsters?

No – it is probably best to avoid adding new hamsters to a colony. They can be territorial and may well attack the new member of the group.

Want to know more about looking after your pet?

The writer of this book, Dr. Gordon Roberts, is a veterinarian and owns a total of eight animal hospitals around the UK. He believes that the key to a healthy, happy pet is preventative care, which is only possible when pet owners take the initiative to educate themselves about their animals. As a result, Gordon has written dozens of useful reports on pet care in order to share his years of experience with discerning pet owners. As a thank you for purchasing this book, you can browse and download his specialist reports completely free of charge! You'll learn all sorts of useful information about how to spot possible health conditions early on, and how to make preventative care for your pet a priority, helping you save time and money on visits to the vet later on. To view and download these bonus reports, simply visit Gordon's website at: http://drgordonroberts.com/freereportsdownload/.

Best wishes,
Gordon

Made in the USA
San Bernardino, CA
29 November 2018